PIANO • VOCAL • GUITAR

TOY STORY 4: Music from the Motion Picture Soundtrack
MUSIC COMPOSED BY RANDY NEWMAN

Disney/Pixar Elements TM & © 2019 Disney/Pixar
All Rights Reserved.

ISBN 978-1-5400-6430-1

Visit Hal Leonard Online at
www.halleonard.com

Contact us:
Hal Leonard
7777 West Bluemound Road
Milwaukee, WI 53213
Email: info@halleonard.com

In Europe, contact:
Hal Leonard Europe Limited
42 Wigmore Street
Marylebone, London, W1U 2RN
Email: info@halleonardeurope.com

In Australia, contact:
Hal Leonard Australia Pty. Ltd.
4 Lentara Court
Cheltenham, Victoria, 3192 Australia
Email: info@halleonard.com.au

CONTENTS

YOU'VE GOT A FRIEND IN ME

Music and Lyrics by
RANDY NEWMAN

Now, some oth-er folks might be a lit-tle bit smart-er than I am,

big-ger and strong-er, too. ___ May-be. But none of them will

ev-er love ___ you the way ___ I do, ___ just me and you, ___ boy.

And as the years go by, ___ our friend-ship will nev-er die. ___

I CAN'T LET YOU THROW YOURSELF AWAY

Music and Lyrics by
RANDY NEWMAN

THE BALLAD OF THE LONESOME COWBOY

Music and Lyrics by
RANDY NEWMAN

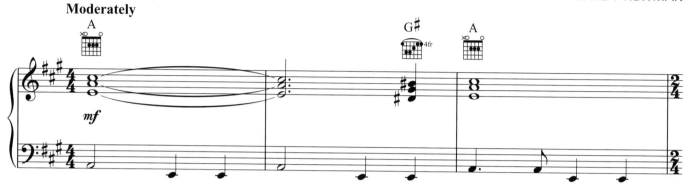

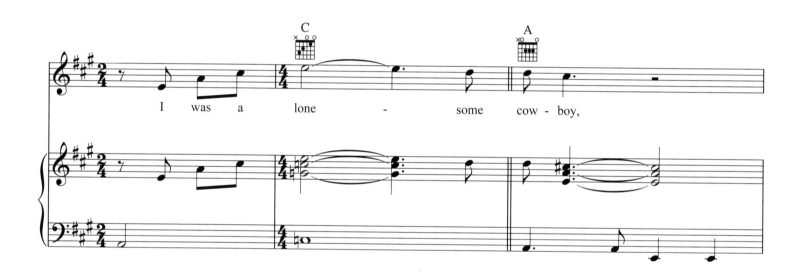

I was a lone - some cow - boy,

lone - some as I could be.

You came a - long,

22

SCHOOL DAZE

Music by
RANDY NEWMAN

TRASH CAN CHRONICLES

Music by
RANDY NEWMAN

Moderately

OPERATION HARMONY

Music by
RANDY NEWMAN

Moderately, in 2

COWBOY SACRIFICE

Music by
RANDY NEWMAN